ENJOY FEASTING ON GOD

One Day at a Time

ROSE
Leibundguth

ENJOY FEASTING ON GOD — *One Day at a Time*

Unless otherwise indicated, all Scripture quotations
are taken from the *King James Version* and the *Amplified Version* of
the Bible.

ENJOY FEASTING ON GOD — *One Day at a Time*

Library of Congress Control Number: 2003093151
ISBN 1-931262-16-0

Copyright © 2003 by Rose Leibundguth
Rose Leibundguth Ministries
Burgin, Kentucky 40310

Printed in the United States of America. All rights reserved under
International Copyright Law. Contents and/or cover may not be
reproduced in whole or in part in any form without the express written
consent of the Publisher.

Published by
Rose Leibundguth Ministries
Burgin, Kentucky 40310

Introduction

Psychology, psychiatry, sociology, science tells us there are many "truths" ... such as gravity, math, chemical combinations, just to name a few. This book represents a supernatural help to all people who are searching for love, peace, joy ... and "THE Truth"! God's Word is the Truth ... supernatural truth.

Mixing hope, joy and faith from God's Word with understanding and speaking His Word out of your mouth, applies God's Truth to every circumstance in your life. You can have confidence in the integrity of God's Word to diligently stand in His Truth — His Word and His Love — Jesus.

The purpose of this book is to reveal Jesus to you! With His principles from God's Word ... Jesus will instruct you in how to cooperate with *and* apply God's Word to your life to walk free ... to walk in joy ... free from fear, defeat, worry, despair ... Satan's attacks.

Many people today are seeking freedom ... freedom from physical, emotional, financial and mental suffering! But they talk and walk in fear, doubt, worry, unbelief and failure until they establish that image in their mind and heart. Their thoughts and words and actions produce a vivid blueprint that cripple and limit them.

In the following pages you will learn how to make your blueprint line up with the *unlimited* powerful Word of God.

God is *unlimited* ... His victorious, unlimited power is for you!

Enjoy Feasting on God
One Day at a Time

JESUS IS LOVE

~

" ... For (during) forty days in the wilderness (desert), where He was tempted (tried, tested exceedingly) by the devil. And He ate nothing during those days, and when they were completed, He was hungry. Then the devil said to Him, 'If you are God's Son, command these stones to be made (loaves of) bread'. And Jesus said, 'It is written, Man shall not live and be upheld and sustained by (on) bread alone, but by every word that comes forth from the mouth of God'."
Luke 4:2-4

Beloved, Jesus was hungry! Without food, Jesus had spent 40 days and 40 nights in the wilderness (desert) where He was tried *exceedingly* by the devil!

Now the devil challenged Jesus *and* God! The body of Jesus hungered for physical food! Yet, Jesus filled to over flowing ... over flowing ... with joy and love and confidence in His Father!

Jesus is confident in every Word of His Father God!
Jesus knows Satan!
He knows Satan is His enemy!
The devil *is* the exceeding Tempter!
The Tempter, the devil (Satan) ...
will always try to tempt us by aiming
at what he *thinks* is our deepest weakness!

SATAN IS THE TEMPTER!

But, Satan is defeated!   Colossians 2:15

" *... weeping may endure for a night, but joy cometh in the morning."* (KJV)   Psalms 30:5

You see, if you're a person who walks in faith, it won't matter how dark the world gets ... it won't matter how dark circumstances seem right now ... you are rest assured that God's Word in Psalms 30:5 is the truth and a bright day of *joy* is on the way!

The devil can't keep up any attack that he gets going! He doesn't have the power to do so. Finally he will give up and crawl off in his own defeat! That's why you understand that the force of *joy* keeps you strong and you will outlast the devil!

Paul spoke about this in Galatians 5:22-23 when he listed *joy* as a fruit of the Spirit and went on to say,
" ... against such there is no law."

That's right! There isn't one force ... in existence ... that can rise up and overcome the power of the fruit of joy ... or any other fruit of the Spirit!

Paul also included other valuable fruits of the Spirit on his list like "love" ... but I want you to start thinking about "joy" here!

I know that you can see at that desert edge, with the agony of hunger tearing at the body and mind of Jesus, as Satan relentlessly tempted Him ... that Jesus was joyful as He made a godly decision!

Jesus had to decide whether to be despaired and listen to the devil asking Him to prove that He was God's Son ... by turning rocks into bread ... then eat — OR ... Jesus could decide to make a joyful, Word of God decision!

Jesus made a godly decision! He decided to feast on Father God ... to feast on His Father's Word! He decided to meditate ... to submit to ... to agree with ... to stand on ... to joyfully speak out God's powerful Word and resist the devil's temptation!

The joy for Jesus is in His Father's Word! He knows that the devil is twisted ... perverted ... and anything that is twisted is weaker than it's original beginning.

> **God's Spirit is full of His Glory and full of His joy!**

Jesus knows that when God and His Spirit come on the scene ... twisted hate has to yield to love ... twisted fear has to yield to faith ... and joy will whip the tar out of weakness and despair every time!

Jesus decided to boldly speak out Father God's written Word from His heart — His Spirit.

Remember, the devil had been *exceedingly* trying and testing Jesus for 40 long days *and* 40 nights.

In that enduring 40 day time, we can imagine that Jesus had every opportunity offered to Him to fall into morbid grief which is the opposite of God's glory and joy!

According to the Greek translation ... to be filled with God's *glory* is to be *"heavy laden with every thing that is good"* ... to be filled with *grief* is to be *"heavy laden with everything that is bad"*.

Now, after 40 tormenting days and nights, the devil aimed at the agonizing, hunger needs of Jesus and he proudly challenged Jesus to turn rocks into bread to eat ... to turn His back on God's glory!

The physical, emotional needs of Jesus were tremendous! Yet, His Spirit was filled with God's Glory!

Have you ever faced such a temptation — a circumstance as this? Have there been ... are there now situations or circumstances in your life that seem physically, mentally, emotionally or spiritually unbearable?

I know there have been times in my life ... mental ... health ... emotional ... financial ... all of which looked like in the natural they might end up sinking me like a wrecked burning ship!

The devil tempts us to throw down our joy, our love, our trust in God ... he tempts us to give up ... tempts us to rely on ourselves instead of God ... tempts us to turn our back against Jesus ... tempts us to ignore God's Holy Son and His powerful Word ... tempts us to yield to the flesh, to the natural, and turn a hard rock circumstance into a bread feast!

Every breathing child of God has had this opportunity offered to them to give up — quit — to look to themselves ... to look only at their circumstances and ask themselves, *"Am I going to believe in Jesus ... line up my thoughts and actions with God and believe my Father and His Word to provide for me?*

OR, am I going to ignore God's Word and listen only to my feelings ... my fears ... and my thoughts?

What am I going to look at and go by ... God — and His Word? Or am I going to look at only what I can physically see or emotionally feel?"

People decide and make choices every day!

**Today — now ...
YOU can decide *to* decide ...
to enjoy feasting on God *in His Word*!**

The only successful, great choice and decision for Jesus to make, as His body hungered at that desert edge, was that He believe and speak His Father God's Word!

Then Jesus joyfully stood firm … on God's Words … over what felt like … seemed like … unbearable, agonizing circumstances. He gave Satan no permission!

Give the devil *no* permit to kill!

Jesus decided! He gave the devil *no* permission to kill His trust in God. Jesus knew that the joy and glory of God is more powerful than any opportunity or grief the devil could dream up.

Jesus knew that disabling grief is demonic — that it is the very opposite to God's glory! He knew that He better not start grieving over His circumstances or His hunger — He knew better than to listen to Satan tempt Him to prove Himself — to exercise His power — to consider eating for one single moment!

The devil challenged Jesus — challenged God — to look at His body screaming for food — to start proving that He was God's powerful Son!

Jesus decided *not* to look at or act on His feelings!

Confidently … Jesus knows … that the joy and glory of God is His life … His strength … that Father God's life giving word's uphold and sustain you!

Jesus decided to feast on God!

Beloved, as you trust God ... as you *speak* God's Words of Life over your circumstances ... *speaking* God's Word becomes a literal feast to your body, your mind and your spirit ... just like good ole' fresh hot bread, butter and jelly can be to your physical body!

"You are snared with the words of your lips, you are caught by the speech of your mouth." Proverbs 6:2

**You see, words are either words of life ...
or words of death ... or idle words!**
Deuteronomy 8:3; Proverbs 18:21; Matthew 4:4
John 5:24; 6:63; Philippians 2:16

You can trust and you can speak Father God's Words of Life over your every circumstance.

You can stand strong in His Words of joy and faith!

Jesus decided to feast ... to be strong ... on God's Words.

Honey, we are in the final hours of God's plans!

Right now, God is giving us the physical, mental and spiritual strength to stand and rise up in the complete ability of God's glory ... completely healed, completely delivered, completely prosperous ... and completely prepared for the return of Jesus according to His divine plan!

God is asking us to *receive* Him in all His glory.

> **"He brought them forth with silver and gold ... not one feeble person ... He brought forth His people with joy ... ."** Psalms 105

Beloved, God wants us strong ... just like Jesus ... to confidently stand in His joy ... to be in His Glory ... able to stand strong enough in His Word to carry out His final hour plans.

God wants us reaping His final harvest and going out of here in the rapture with Him rich in the glorious victory and joy that he intends.

When Jesus returns, God doesn't want a bunch of whipped wimps crawling off this earth in defeat and disgrace ... filled with disease and despair!

We are going to leave this earth in greater glory than every Israelite did when they left Egypt. And if you think that wasn't God's glory then read all of Psalms 105:37-43.

"He brought them forth also with silver and gold: and there was not one feeble person among their tribes. Egypt was glad when they departed: for the fear of them fell upon them. He spread a cloud for a covering; and fire to give light in the night. The people *asked, and He brought quails, and satisfied them with the bread of heaven. He opened the rock, and the waters gushed out; it ran in the dry places like a river. For He remembered His holy word and promise to Abraham His servant. And He brought forth His people with joy, and His chosen ones with gladness and singing."* (KJV; AMP)

Beloved, I have learned that God does what He says ... joy heals ... God says that He brought forth His people healed with joy!

I speak to you about this direct from experience!

There was a time in my life when I was guilt ridden, spiritually and mentally ignorant ... physically sick ... emotionally and financially a wreck! I was a sinking ship on a raging high sea of despair and defeat! My life was filled with disease ... filled with words of fear, worry and defeat!

I was joy-less — sick and despaired in every way! I was broke financially ... in debt beyond natural belief or recovery!

Then God's Word began to root deep into my heart ... I saw it! Proverbs 17:22, *"A happy heart is good medicine and a cheerful mind works healing ... ."*

Joy and healing are connected ... science has even proven this with laughter bringing about medical results that bring healing in the body!

God's Word is a feast of joy!

Remember, Jesus decided to feast on His Father's joyous Word! Jesus knows that He can trust His Father!

Jesus *expected*!
He *expected* **Father God to abundantly** *and* **correctly feed Him mentally ... physically ... emotionally ... and spiritually!**

**Jesus *expected* ... He *required* His Father
to meet His every need!**

Remember, as physically hungry as Jesus was, He boldly told the devil, *"Man does not live by bread alone but will "live" be upheld and sustained by every Word from God's mouth!"*

Words are serious business!

Jesus boldly spoke Deuteronomy 8:3 to the devil!

You might say, *"Well Rose, Jesus is the Son of God. He was able to speak God's Word and resist the temptations of the devil because He's Jesus!"*

Your right! This is true! Jesus is The Son of God.

And, holy child of God, just like Jesus, through the power of God His Father ... God says that *we too are **His beloved Sons and Daughters***!

As God's holy child, God's Word says that YOU are to stop — speak His Word — and resist the devil! YOU can submit to the glory of God!

"So be subject to God. Resist the devil (stand firm against him), and he will flee from you."
John 1:12, 13; Romans 8:14
2 Corinthians 6:18; Galatians 4:5, 6, 7; James 4:7

God is our loving Lord ... our Father ... our Rescuer! We are His beloved, godly, holy children ... His beloved Sons and Daughters!

" ... the Lord knows how to rescue the godly out of temptations and trials ... !"   2 Peter 2:9

The Lord knows how to rescue you, His godly child, with His Word ... in His authority ... and in His victorious ability!

But, YOU have to decide! You have to decide to not allow Satan to sneak up on you!

> **BE like Jesus ...**
> **joyfully confess God's Word**
> **and watch Him work!**

Stop the devil from talking louder to you than your joy or talking louder than your faith Words of God can talk!

Decide now, just like Jesus decided, that you are going to joyfully *speak* God's Word loud and clear ... right in the face of your every circumstance!

Why, I remember a time when people thought that the more stricken with sorrow and grief you were in life and during church ... the more spiritual you were. I found out that is not the truth.

God is so full of joy ... Jesus is so full of joy. It is time, as God's children, that we are going to totally follow Jesus and receive that we are to be full of His joy!

Before I learned God's Word on what I am telling you ... mostly around my loved ones ... I was a griever ... a screamer ... a whiner ... a fit thrower ... a bawler and a squawler ... a fear talker ... a worrier! Or, I would freeze the world out with my silence. On "better" days, my life still was not based on God's Word! Each day was guided by circumstances ... by the strength of how I *felt* — or often my life was led by what other people thought or what other people said ... not what Ephesians 4 says!

It takes great strength to shut out the hustle-bustle of the world and live by faith! The Lord Jesus has taught me that you can't live by faith without joy.

" ... the joy of the Lord is (our) strength."
Nehemiah 8:10

JOY ... joy ... joy! JOY in His Lordship ... joy in His love ... joy in His mercy and grace ... joy in the Lord *is* total strength ... your total strength! This is the most exciting good news ever!

Paul prayed for the Colossians to be *"strengthened with all might, according to (God's) glorious power, unto all patience and longsuffering with joyfulness."*
Colossians 1:11

Beloved, decide today to stop the devil from keeping you ignorant of Father's joy, His strength, His glorious power ... and His Word for you!

Paul knew the importance of joy! He knew God's strength ... your strength in Jesus ... is joined and connected to joy!

Paul was saying we are strengthened with all might with God's glorious joyfulness!

Start *agreeing* with God's Word today! Start *disagreeing* with the devil!

Stop him from robbing you of Father's victorious Word available to you. Stop allowing God's glorious Word, already living inside you, to be quiet!

"And this is the confidence (the assurance, the privilege of boldness) which we have in Him: (we are sure) that if we ask anything (make any request) according to His will (in agreement with His own plan), He listens to and hears us!" 1 John 5:14

You can confidently, BOLDLY SPEAK OUT in prayer ... in Jesus ... in His Name! Find God's Word over your particular situation! Joyfully, boldly begin PRAYING GOD'S WORD out loud over your situation! God listens to you — God hears you!

Therefore, holy beloved, be bold! What you say in prayer is the key to getting your prayers answered. You must first communicate to God in faith believing what He has already communicated to you from His Word ... fully confident and expecting that your Word of God prayers will have results.

You can apply faith pressure and joy to your circumstances!

Apply *faith* pressure ... apply *joy* pressure!

Apply God's joy, love and faith to your life just like His love and faith is applied to Jesus!

God's power in His Word is *for you* and it is no less for you than it is to Jesus! Absolutely not!

" ... let us hold fast (hold firmly) to our profession, our confession of faith without wavering; (for He is faithful Who gave us the promises)." Hebrews 10:23

You can hold fast, without wavering, to the faithfulness of God! Oh yes, beloved ... I can assure you, God is faithful and you can hold fast to Him!

You can hold fast to His faith filled Word. Father God is a faith loving God ... He is *full and overflowing* with faith! God promised us His faith when He gave us Jesus!

God sows His Word seeds of faith and strength deep into our hearts — sown into the rich ground of our new, re-born, re-created spirits ... *in Jesus ... by Jesus ... through Jesus.*

God is faithful! As we joyfully speak His faithful Words — our minds then become His new ... re-newed ... re-created ... minds.

It is our choice, our decision, to work *with* God to make the things we desire come to pass. It is up to us to *receive ... to receive ... to receive!*

It is up to us to give ... to give ... to give Jesus ... to honor God ... to glorify God!

We can choose when we will hold fast to speak words of joy, faith and love! Or, we can choose to speak and follow words of fear, worry, doubt, hate and unbelief!

Talk to God ... ask of Him with your godly heart ... not with wrong purposes or evil selfish motives. James 4:3

CONFESS HIS WORD! When you diligently seek the Lord and continue confessing and seeding His words of love, joy and faith over your life ... God will richly reward your efforts. Hebrews 11:6

You see, Satan will always attempt to rob you; to steal from you ... to steal God's Word from you — to steal from you God's very seeds of His joy ... His life giving words ... and His love!

Satan has been stealing for centuries and he isn't about to stop trying now!

Satan *(your enemy)* wants to steal your joy of the Lord Jesus ... because he knows the joy of the Lord is your strength!

The enemy attempts ... tries you ... tries to get you to doubt Jesus ... to speak words of fear or chit-chat or misery or worry or defeat in every circumstance of your life in order to kill and steal your joy ... to kill God's Word from your heart and steal His Word out of your mouth!

The defeated devil *(the defeated enemy)*, tries to steal your joy ... your life strength! The devil will try to steal from you just like he tried to steal from Jesus at that desert edge!

"Death and life are in the power of the tongue, and they who indulge in it shall eat the fruit of it (for death or life) ... For by your words you will be justified and acquitted and by your words you will be condemned and sentenced."   Proverbs 18:21; Matthew 12:37

**God's Word's are your power keys ...
You have God's Word power keys ...
to use ...
to *bind* and to *loose*!**
Matthew 16:19

You have His very Keys of Life and Death in the power of your tongue ... the very Keys to the Kingdom of Life are in your mouth!

You are God's beloved child ... as the beloved child of The Most High King ... you have your Father God's Word power keys!

In the joy of the Lord you can stand up and use them!

As God's child ... stand with Jesus ... never, ever again, accept words of fear and doubt or worry to enter into your heart ... to come from your mouth!

I know you can see now why your words and joy of Jesus is so major a force in your life! If you're going to take part in the end-time move of God ... joy is going to have to come all over you and out of your mouth.

God wants your heart grounded and rooted in His love ... strengthened with His might ... by His Spirit ... in your inner man. He wants His Anointed One ... Jesus ... and His Anointing ... dwelling strong in your heart by faith in joy.

God wants you rooted and grounded, like never before, in Jesus! He wants His joy and love so deep within you that you can comprehend the breadth and length and depth and height of His love Jesus and His Anointing. This is a love that passes all knowledge ... that you might be filled with all the fullness of God! Ephesians 3:16-19

Use God's power Word keys to flip His faith switch on high! Then, watch Him turn up His power high over your life! You'll get to see the devil run and watch your circumstances change!

The devil runs when he sees that you understand your strength comes from knowing that your joy and faith is in Jesus ... that the joy of your Lord makes you strong.

You may not think that you have any joy in your heart right now! You may be feeling joy-less!

But, let me assure you, as a born-again child of God, you have the joy of Jesus living in your spirit. You just need to begin to praise God and get that joy stirred up to start flowing.

You can purpose in your heart to stir up your joy of the Lord! Just like an old water pump needs primed to get the flow of water going ... prime your joy pump in praise.

Are your words joyful ...
faithful — or fretful — worried and fearful?

Let's get rid of fretful, worried and fearful words by giving *all* praise to Jesus, our promised Highest Love ... our Savior and Lord ... our abundant Protector and Provider!

Start right now praising the Lord Jesus! Praise Him that in His power *by His faith in you* ... you *refuse* to listen to the defeated devil ever again! Determine that you are going to receive and walk praising God for His blessings for you!

YOU absolutely *refuse* to allow Satan to rob you of any blessings of God over your life ... any further!

Your enemy ... Satan ... won't *and* he can't steal, kill and destroy from your life ... *if you don't let him!*

PRAY! Use these seven scripture guides to exercise God's fearless Word power!

With God you can make prayer work over every circumstance in your life!

Always remember ... when you meditate on the Word of God ... revelation will begin to rise in your heart ... joy follows ... PRAYER WORKS!

> **Joy follows because you gain a deep knowledge of Father God.**

Joy follows as you praise God and you become confident in being able to be right in the throne room of God by prayer! Because you know God hears you and He answers you ... you will rejoice!

Let's go over these seven powerful steps of prayer God showed me to use in His Word!

PRAYER WORKS :

1. **Speak God's Word, the answer,** *not* **the problem!**
   Isaiah 55:11

2. **Apply faith** *and* **joy pressure!**
   Psalms 63:1-8; Hebrews 10:23

3. **Never ever accept fear or doubt!**
   Ephesians 6:11; 2 Corinthians 10:5

4. **Visualize success** *and* **reject failure!**   Psalms 107:2

5. **Testify what you believe!**   John 14:13, 14

6. **Be a blessing!**   Galatians 6:2

7. **Love ... give ...** *and* **you will receive!**
   Luke 6:38; James 5:16

Remember, Satan tries you! He will always try you! Satan tries to seduce you — but only *with* your submission *to* him and *in y*our agreement *with* him is he ever able to get you into doubt or unbelief by speaking words in an attitude of fear, worry, depression or defeat!

I have come to understand that to live victoriously we *have to* get into God's Word ... and keep His Word before our ears and eyes ... *guard* our hearts ... meditate on His Words day and night!   Proverbs 4:20-23

Just look at some of what Jesus said to us and to His disciples just a few hours before He went to the cross at Calvary to shed His blood for us!

"If you live in Me (abide vitally united to Me) and My words remain in you and continue to live in your hearts, ask whatever you will, and it shall be done for you ...

If you keep my commandments (if you continue to obey My instructions), you will abide in My love and live on in it, just as I have obeyed My Father's commandments and live on in His love. I have told you these things, that My joy and delight may be in you, and that your joy and gladness may be of full measure and complete and overflowing ...

but now ask and keep on asking and you will receive, so that your joy (gladness, delight) may be full and complete." John 15:7, 10, 11; 16:24

We can truly live in God's love ... *receive* His rich blessings ... richly live ... filled to over flowing in His joy ... full and complete!

I am completely convinced ... I am totally confident to walk in agreement with these words of God from Jesus ... *and* with James 3:2-7 ... simply put, this scripture says that *by the words of our mouth, lined up with the powerful Word of God, walking in God's wisdom and the Holy Spirit,* we can set people who are held captive, free from all bondages ... we can set people free to love, to live, to give, to have His joy — to have life abundantly in Jesus in His Name!

If you have been fearful ... agonizing over a lost or a wandering loved one ... you can replace your agonizing thoughts.

Exchange your agonizing, worried thinking by standing on God's promise in Isaiah 54:13, *" ... all your (spiritual) children shall be disciples (taught by the Lord and obedient to His will), and great shall be the peace and undisturbed composure of your children."*

Beloved, you can rejoice! When you start praising God, standing on Him in His Word instead of crying over what you see the devil doing to that loved one, you will start shouting in joy about what God has already done ... and can do ... on their behalf!

Honey, choose to stand only in the promises of God! This choice brings you to a place of peace and utter joy.

Tell the devil, *"Forget it ... I am standing on my Father's Word that all victory is already won for my loved one. In fact, all of my loved ones shall be taught by the Lord ... and great shall be the peace and undisturbed composure of all my loved ones!"*

If the devil doesn't gladly stop there but keeps on pressing in on you with doubts like how sorry you should be about your loved ones conditions ... again, remind him of Isaiah 53:4, *" ... Jesus bore all my griefs and sorrows ... ."*

God is obligated to perform His Word on your behalf.
Jeremiah 1:12; Ezekiel 12:25
Isaiah 44:26; 42:6, 7; 55:11; Luke 1:20, 37

Tell the devil you have no grief or sorrows, according to Isaiah 53:3-5! Say, *"Now it's my decision to rejoice in Jesus and what a good time I'm going to have!"*

OR, beloved, you can go backwards and choose to set worlds on fire with curses, fears, worry and doubt!

OR, with God's Words of joy and hope ... faith and love ... stand up and extinguish every fiery dart and flame!

Start out by taking baby steps. Then move on into walking ... then running. God will strengthen you.

He will build you up to your running strength and confidence in speaking His Word ... *as you speak!*

Remember, when you speak words of fear or doubt and unbelief ... as you listen to or act (walk) with the devil ... you are listening to and walking with The Thief, The Killer, The Destroyer!

Just like Jesus did, without any fear ... joyfully refuse the temptation of the enemy and begin speaking and giving God's powerful Word!

Speak GOD's WORD in love and joy over your every circumstance!

The book of Proverbs is full of God's joyful Words.

"A man has joy in making an apt answer, and a word spoken at the right moment—how good it is ... The mind of the (uncompromisingly) righteous studies how to answer ... He hears the prayer of the (consistently) righteous ... The light in the eyes (of him whose heart is joyful) rejoices the hearts of others, and good news nourishes the bones."   Proverbs 15:23, 28, 29, and 30

Examine God's Word! Examine your words! Words are actions! Examine your actions! REJOICE! Watch your joy rejoice the hearts of others ... good news nourishes!

At all costs, be a blessing!

Make your words and actions match up to God's Words!

Jesus said, *"I will give you the keys of the kingdom of heaven; and whatever you bind (declare to be improper and unlawful) on earth must be what is already bound in heaven; and whatever you loose (declare lawful) on earth must be what is already loosed in heaven."* Matthew 16:19

> *In Jesus*, **God has given you His power ... His Word keys of the kingdom of heaven!**

You have *HIS WORDS* ... His very *Keys*
of the kingdom of heaven ...

You have God's power Word Keys to use ...

Jesus said you can bind *and* loose ...
with your mouth ...
everything that is already bound ...
and everything that is already loosed in heaven!

You hold His very Keys
of **Life** (love *and* joy) or **Death** (fear *and* hate)
in your mouth!

You have the ability (power) *in Jesus* ... with your mouth ... to bind poverty, sickness, disease, defeat, fear, depression, worry ... you can bind every evil and negative force from your life on this earth! Because these things are absolutely already bound in heaven.

You have the ability (power) *in Jesus* ... to loose every good thing of God for your life ... faith, prosperity, divine health, a sound mind, wisdom, love, joy, peace ... every godly, positive force ... filled to over flowing with the joy of the Lord!

You can loose the goodness of God and the authority of Jesus on this earth ... because these things are absolutely already loose in heaven!

> **God's Words ... are rivers of Life, Health and Prosperity flowing from your mouth!**

> **God knows you can swim with Him!**

As a little child I began to absolutely love the water ... streams, rivers, lakes, the ocean. But, I couldn't swim.

One day I was with a dear friend of my family at their swimming pool. All of a sudden he picked me up and threw me out into the deep water up over my head.

As I flew through the air I heard him say, *"Sink or swim Rose Mary ... sink or swim ... I know you can do it ... I know you can do it!"*

Now this may sound drastic, but, I also trusted ... I had confidence in my friend that was standing ready to rescue me if need be! My friend knew me well enough that when that big day came for me to go into the deep water ... he knew I would swim!

Not only did I swim in that deep water that day ... but, I went on to learn more ... to water ski ... dive ... perform water ballet ... train and work as a life-guard ... swim long distances ... learn to scuba dive ... go sailing and boating in the ocean!

By the time I was 19 years old ... I became a great swimmer ... totally confident ... ! One day, without any fear or concern ... I immediately swam out beyond a mile into an early morning, treacherous ocean tide to save a drowning little girl that was swept out by the currents.

Now, did I start out by being able to swim that well, and being able to save that drowning child? No, no, no!

But I did start somewhere! Back when I was a little child ... growing up in Kentucky in the heat of the summer ... I would walk along the Big Sandy river bank ... sticking my big toe in that Kentucky river's cool mucky edge!

You see, that one day came ... years later ... when that little girl in the ocean would have drowned if I hadn't been ready ... been prepared to swim! And oh the joy I still have today as I remember the love from her parents in a letter praising God and thanking me for saving their child's life!

Today, swimming in the ocean, watching my grandchildren learn to love the water is a glorious joy for me. Today, all my grown daughters and their husbands are great swimmers ... water skiers ... now, all of my six grandchildren are being taught and learning how to love the water and swim!

With my husband David, (who was a professional diver when we first met), I have the greatest fun ever when he takes me diving into deep ocean waters and teaches me about the joy of God's beautiful creations.

First hand ... the tremendous beauty of all God's sea creatures ... underwater up close ... is hard to describe!

You see, with correct knowledge ... you are easily prepared for deep water! With great respect for the water ... I have learned to never be *fear-ful,* but to be respectful, of the deepest of waters!

I praise God that through the years I have been able to develop the knowledge and strength to swim for miles for hours at a time! I joyfully swim in places I go all over the world.

This is all just like our Father God! God knows you!

Beloved, God knows His creation! Before the beginning of time you were *with Him* ... YOU were given His Spirit and YOU have His Spirit ... YOU can walk ... YOU can confidently run in the depths of highest victory *with Him* with His Spirit living inside you!

"Before I formed you in the womb I knew (and) approved of you (as My chosen instrument), and before you were born I separated and set you apart, consecrating you; (and) I appointed you as a prophet to the nations."   Jeremiah 1:5; Isaiah 49:5; Romans 8:29

God knew you before you were formed in your mother's womb ... before you were born ... He approved of you (as His chosen instrument) ... He set you apart ... He created you before the beginning of time to learn to walk ... to run ... to flow deeply *with Him* as His life to nations!

God daily prepares you with His correct knowledge to speak and to stand ... to walk ... to run confidently WITH HIM ... to run in the *unlimited* depths of His powerful Word ... in His Son's love, His joy!

There is the greatest joy in learning to walk ... to run *with* Father God — to completely trust in Him in His Son Jesus!

Beloved, it is time! It is time to swim into God's deepest waters of His joy ... His glory ... and His Word with Jesus! It is time to take Him to all nations.

In praise and thanksgiving ... it is time we deeply fellowship with God in His Word and in the power of His Holy Spirit! It is time to receive *all* of God ... to rejoice and to praise the Lord across this earth!

It is time! It is time to *receive and rejoice* in Jesus!

**Praising Him everyday ...
ALL day,
can start NOW ... today!**

You may start out thinking you can't ... you may think you don't have anything to thank God for — but if you'll hang in there — quickly, you will find out that you do!

Decide today! Start out by thanking Him for the precious blood of Jesus that washed away every sin you ever had! Thank Him, that because of Jesus, you are going to be with Him in heaven!

Thank Him that He loves you even when you think you might drown as everything around you feels like a final disaster and you don't understand!

Start shouting, rejoicing out loud today, *"I thank you God that you have washed away my sins and you love me!"*

Right about now, I know you might be saying, *"Well, Rose this is easy for you to say because you are able to be more outspoken than I am ... you don't know my circumstances or understand, I don't feel like I can do this!"*

Honey, you're right, I don't know your circumstances. But, I do know Jesus! And I know that how you *feel* has nothing to do with this!

You don't have to *feel* like rejoicing in order to rejoice!

That is another lie of the devil ... telling you to wait until you feel like rejoicing to do it! As a matter of fact, God and joy are bigger than any feelings or emotions or limits or circumstances you will ever have!

David, in Psalms 27:8, told the Lord, ***"You have said, Seek My face (inquire for and require My presence as your vital need). My heart says to You, Your face (Your presence), Lord, will I seek, inquire for, and require (of necessity and on the authority of Your Word)."***

You see, *requiring* God's presence ... *trusting* God ... *living* in God's Word ... *rejoicing* ... are decisions ... acts of your will.

> **God wants you to seek His face ... inquire for and require His presence as your vital need!**

> **Seek —
> make God's presence
> on the authority of His Word ...
> and joy in Him ...
> your vital need!**

When times come that you don't think you can rejoice ... when you don't feel like rejoicing or being joyful ... just sail on out into the deepest water of God's love and set your will to rejoice as you *require* Him in the authority of His Word to hold you up!

Stir up your joy of the Lord. Get that joy to flowing!

God won't let you sink! He will teach you how to confidently swim safely in the deepest of waters with Him!

Jesus said in Matthew 6:33, *"Seek ye first the kingdom of God and His righteousness and all these things shall be added unto you."* (KJV)

Oh Yes, holy beloved … Jesus taught that God already knows what you need … He already has His every good plan set and He is your abundant "need Meeter"!

Are you having a financial problem right now? Are you worrying about a relationship … a husband … a wife … a child … ? Are you anxious … about tomorrow … about your health … your job … your business … your ministry … your future?

Maybe you think or you feel like you don't even have a future!

Well, let me tell you! If you can't sleep … if you have no peace … no hope … no joy … instead of staying up all night worrying or spending all day fretting … **start praising God!**

Start praising God by humming … singing … by shouting God's Word out loud in the night.

Start laughing at the devil and keep laughing! Keep laughing until daylight dawns … and joy comes! Jesus knows what's going on in your life!

> Jesus knows you … He prays for you …
> He knows that Father God
> has nothing but good answers
> and good plans for you!

The Spirit of Jesus is full of the joy and glory of God!

He is joyful ... for you!

Jesus, after praying to His Father, said to Peter in Luke 22:31-32, " ... *LISTEN! Satan has asked excessively that (all of) you be given up to him (out of the power and keeping of God), that he might sift (all of) you like grain, but I have prayed especially for you (Peter), that your (own) faith may not fail; and when you yourself have turned again, strengthen and establish your brethren.*"

Stop! Speak this scripture slowly ... again ... out loud! Jesus said, " ... *I have prayed ... !*" I know you see Jesus using God's powerful words to resist the excessive, persistence of the enemy!

I know you can see the importance *for you* to diligently **read** ... **believe** ... **receive** ... **agree** with ... **understand** ... **speak** ... and **act** on God's powerful Word for yourself!

Satan asked *excessively* to sift us ALL ... to sift every human being on this planet earth until the end of the ages!

The devil asked *excessively* **that** *all* **of us be given to him out of the power and keeping of God, so that he could** *sift* **us all like grain, measure us out ...** *and* **mark us all off!**

The devil wants to sift us like grain ... sift means to measure out ... to weigh us out ... to mark us off! Satan wants to mark us all off!

But — Jesus prayed!

As that final crucifixion hour was closing in on Jesus ... JESUS PRAYED *and* HE PRAISED ... He rejoiced ... He talked to Father God about us from His Word!

Jesus prayed ... that the power and glory of God *keep* ALL of us!

Honey, Jesus prayed, *" ... that (our) faith may not fail ... !"* This prayer that our faith would not fail is answered for you ... it is powerfully answered for *all* mankind! But, we have to *receive*!

Jesus knows the devil! He knows that He permanently defeated and paralyzed him!

Jesus *prays ... we pray ... Father God listens!*

The devil can not ... is not able ... not allowed ... to sift us ... *unless WE let him*!

Earlier Jesus told Peter, *" ... Peter, you will deny Me three times."*

You see, Jesus knew Peter! Jesus knew all about Peter! He knew what Peter would do before Peter did it!

Jesus already knows us! He knows our circumstances ... He knows what all of us can *and* will do before we do it! This is good!

God gave us Jesus! Jesus knows that we have His heart ... His Mind!

God knows all about our circumstances! He knows because He is always with us every hour ... every day ... until the end of the ages!
Matthew 28:20; 1 Corinthians 2:16; 11:3: Philippians 2:5

"You know my downsitting and my uprising; You understand my thought afar off ... You are acquainted with all my ways ... For there is not a word in my tongue (still unuttered), but, behold, O Lord, You know it altogether ... You have laid Your hand upon me ... Where could I go from Your Spirit? Or where could I flee from Your presence? If I ... dwell in the uttermost parts of the sea, even there shall Your hand lead me, and Your right hand shall hold me ... ." Psalms 139

I'll always remember the first time I read Psalms 139! As I jumped and shouted I nearly threw my Bible in the air! I saw it ... I understood ... that God knows *everything* about me! He truly means that He is *always* with me. This is the most humbling and exciting experience.

Beloved, God's presence is always with you ... knows all about you ... and He knows all that you will do before you do it.

> **God knows everything about every thing *and* every body!**

s a believer, God's presence *in Jesus* lives *in you*! Jesus wants you to know that you can trust Him ... that you can totally trust yourself *in Him*!

Jesus wants you to know yourself *in Him* ... in the same victorious loving way that He knows you!

**Jesus wants you to know yourself ...
the loving, powerful way
that He knows you!**

You can do *all* things *with Him* and *through Him*!
Philippians 4:13

And, Jesus wants you to know *all* that He has already done *for you*!

Jesus wants you to *know* Him!

Jesus wants you to know that He has already provided His *unlimited* abilities *for* you ... and *in* you!

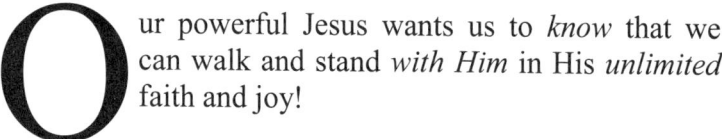ur powerful Jesus wants us to *know* that we can walk and stand *with Him* in His *unlimited* faith and joy!

We can walk without fear of anybody or anything!

Jesus wants us to *know* that we can confidently trust Him to safely guide us ... set us free from distress' and lead us on into His victory in *every* circumstance of our lives!
Psalms 4

" ... You have freed me when I was hemmed in and enlarged me when I was in distress ... But know that the Lord has set apart for Himself (and given distinction to) him who is godly (the man of loving kindness). The Lord listens and heeds when I call to Him."   Psalms 4:1, 3

The Lord knows that we are godly — set free by Him ... enlarged ... set apart for Himself ... He listens and heeds when we call ... we can step out in total confidence *in Him*!

The devil is the complete opposite ... he wants to confuse you ... he wants to disable you ... shrink you down to kill you! Satan is THE Confuser *and* THE Killer!

Jesus said, " *... I HAVE PRAYED especially for you Peter that your (own) FAITH may NOT FAIL; and when you yourself HAVE TURNED again, STRENGTHEN and ESTABLISH your BRETHREN.*"
Luke 22:32

Stop! Speak that scripture out loud! LISTEN to Jesus! Jesus was talking to Father God about Peter *and* about you!

God listens! He listens to Jesus ... *and* He listens to you!

As Jesus was praying to Father God about Peter ... He was also praying about us ... He was planting His Word seeds of instructions on His love deep into the heart of mankind!

Jesus seeds, plants and confirms His love and His Word into our hearts!

Not only did Jesus pray *for* Peter, but remember, Jesus had told Peter that (out of fear) Peter would even deny knowing Him three times in one night!

You see, Jesus was completely aware of Peter! He knew Peter's heart ... He knew his natural weakness', his godly strengths *and* He was aware of Peter's faith! Jesus loved Peter and He *knew* Peter's love for Him. Jesus knew *all* about Peter!

Jesus put His faith *in* Peter. Jesus spoke victorious words of faith over Peter. He knew that He could trust Peter to turn to Him!

Jesus knew that Peter could turn and that he would strengthen and establish the brethren!

Remember earlier, Jesus had said that He would build His Church on Peter's faith and love for Him!
Matthew 16:18

Jesus was profoundly telling Peter, *"I already know what you will do Peter ... I know you ... I love you ... now, I want you to know yourself in Me ... I want you to know what you can do and will do with Me!"*

God loves you ... He knows that you are His godly, holy beloved child.

God loves you as much as He loves Jesus!

Jesus loves you just like God loves you!

Peter loved Jesus! Jesus wanted Peter to know that he loved Him!

Jesus wants you to know that you love Him.

God said, *"We love Him, because He first loved us."*
1 John 4:19

Beloved, what an amazing scripture. God says we love Him ... He *knows* that we love Him ... because He first loved us!

Stop! Look back ... diligently speak again, out loud, Luke 22:32! Ask the Holy Spirit to reveal the *unlimited* depth of God's knowledge and love *for you* in this scripture!

God has faith *in you!* He loves you!

Satan wants you to see yourself as broken and hopeless!

God *does not* see you as broken or hopeless!

> **God does not see mankind as broken!**

I know that you see, God does not see mankind as broken!

He sees mankind in vital need of His presence in His Son as Savior and Lord!

God sees His perfect, beautiful creation needing His Son Jesus as Savior ... Lord ... Redeemer ... Provider ... Helper ... Shepherd ... Protector ... Restorer ... Lover ... in the power of the Holy Spirit.

Jesus *sees* and *knows* that you are faithful ... *and* perfect in Father's Eyes!

God sees His beloved, holy, godly children able to be strong *in Jesus* — able through His Sons love to pray and shore up a weak, sick and dying world.

                Genesis 2:18; Psalms 60:12; 146:5, 6
        Matthew 9:7, 8; Mark 2:11; 1 Corinthians 2:4, 5
                  Hebrews 1:3; 13:6; Romans 8:26

"Let us fearlessly and confidently and boldly draw near to the throne of grace, that we may obtain mercy, and find grace to help in good time for every need (appropriate help and well-timed help, coming just when we need it ... So we take comfort and are encouraged and confidently and boldly say, The Lord is my Helper; I will not be seized with alarm (I will not fear or dread or be terrified). What can man do to me?"

                                                Hebrews 4:16; 13:6

You can confidently — boldly draw near — to the throne of grace to find help for every need — just when you need it!

" ... be strong to apprehend and grasp with all the saints (God's devoted people, the experience of that love) what is the breadth and length and height and depth (of it); (that you may really come) to know (practically, through experience for yourselves) the love of Christ, which far surpasses mere knowledge (without experience); that you may be filled (through all your being) unto all the fullness of God (may have the richest measure of the divine Presence, and become a body wholly filled and flooded with God Himself)."

                                                    Ephesians 3:18, 19

God is telling us that He wants us to really come to know, through experience, the profound depth of the love of Christ! Experience for yourself His deep love! Highly, *totally trust Him* ... experience God's holiness in God's heart as you trust Him — filled in all your being with the fullness of God — flooded with God Himself!

Jesus first loved Peter. He knew that Peter deeply loved Him from his heart ... He knew Peter would not fail!

Jesus knew that with Peter's joy *in Him and in His love* — Peter was free — Peter could never fail!

Revelation 1:5, 6

Jesus said, *"Peter, I pray your own faith not fail ...."*

You see Peter, or his faith, could not fail Jesus!

IN CHRIST
there is no failure!

Peter reacted! Out of natural worldly fear feelings and natural mind thinking ... Peter momentarily allowed *his* faith to *weaken!*

PETER, or his faith, or God's faith in Peter DID NOT FAIL!

IN CHRIST you can never fail!

IN CHRIST — *IN God's Word* — there is no failure!

Failure means to fold up, go under, close down, flop!

Peter did not fold up, go under, close down, or flop ... and neither do you!

Look deeper into the natural mind thinking of Peter in Mark 14:71-72 and Luke 22:56-62 ... where Peter, acting in fear, denied even knowing Jesus ... not once ... but three times in one night ... and if that wasn't enough —

"Then he (Peter) commenced invoking a curse on himself (should he not be telling the truth) and swearing, I do not know the Man about Whom you are talking."
Mark 14:71

Peter began swearing and cursing that he didn't even know Jesus! Now beloved, in the natural, how fearful — how bad can it get?

Praise God, now look ahead at what then happened!

"And the Lord turned and looked at Peter. And Peter recalled the Lord's words, how He had told him, Before the cock crows today, you will deny Me thrice. And he went out and wept bitterly (that is, with painfully moving grief)."
Luke 22:61, 62

Jesus was close enough to Peter to look into his eyes ... to see and hear what was going on! Jesus could see and hear Peter cursing and swearing and denying Him!

Beloved, Peter broke down ... wept aloud ... !

Peter was so close to Jesus that he could see the *all* knowing, *all* loving, beautiful, faithful Eyes of the *all* forgiving Jesus as the Savior and Lord of *all* mankind!

Oh beloved, how Peter wept when he recalled the Lord's words!

When Peter looked into those beautiful, loving, forgiving Eyes of Jesus ... when Peter *saw* The Truth ... when he remembered *all* that Jesus had said ... when he remembered how Jesus had prayed ...

... when Peter remembered Jesus' loving Words of faith and trust over him ... when he remembered how deeply Jesus loved him ... when Peter remembered how Jesus knew his heart of love for Him — how forgiving He is at all costs ... when Peter *saw* in his heart and spirit ... the joy and love of the Lord God Almighty ... His Savior and Lord —

Peter wept bitterly ...
(with painfully moving grief he wept ... *and* he turned)!

Peter gloriously turned.

> **When it comes time to turn —**
> **when we** *see* **—**
> **then we'll turn baby ...**
> **we will turn!**

Honey, I know you see that Peter and his faith weakened ... but Peter's faith, or the faith of Jesus in Peter, could never fail.

Remember, and keep on remembering, Jesus had prayed to Father God that Peter's faith ... *and* our faith ... would not fail ... Jesus said, *"... I pray your faith not fail and when you have turned again, strengthen and establish the brethren."* Luke 22:32

When Peter looked — with his spirit —

Peter *saw* Jesus — he *saw* the loving, forgiving, faithful Eyes of Jesus ... he looked and he saw the victorious, *unlimited* love of Jesus! Peter remembered how Jesus had prayed for him ... had prayed for all mankind ... he remembered,

"I pray your faith not fail;
and when you yourself have turned again,
strengthen and establish your brethren ... !"

Holy beloved, Peter turned and he joyously went forth to minister to thousands the love, salvation, Lordship and healing love of Jesus ... the Son of God! He went forth to minister ... to give ... the living Lord of love ... the joyful, faithful forgiving Christ ... to all mankind for all eternity.

Through Peter's message of Jesus, in one day, 3,000 people came to receive their salvation — to receive their eternal life with God in Jesus as Savior and Lord!

The joy and the anointing of God was so great on Peter — that people were raised from the dead — the mere shadow of Peter healed, strengthened and established the brethren just like Jesus said would happen!
Acts 5:15, 16; 9:34, 40, 41; 10:33, 42-44

Oh holy beloved, Peter remembered ... he saw ... he turned ... and he *received!*

Peter *received* the love — the power — the joy of Jesus!

Look back again with me one more time to when Jesus lovingly talked to Peter ... looked at Peter ... in those dark early morning hours while Jesus was on the way to His final hour of crucifixion ... to die ... then victoriously rise from the grave three days later!

As His blessed hour of crucifixion was nearing ... as that horrible time of torture was occurring ... as He was preparing to totally deliver mankind from all darkness — sin, Satan and death — Jesus, in His great love, stopped ... turned ... and lovingly looked at Peter ... *and* He lovingly saw the heart of all mankind! Ephesians 4:8

Oh the greatness ... the *unlimited knowledge and love* our Lord Jesus has for all of us.

Jesus *knew* that Peter would experience God's great full plan of His saving, total love ... for himself and for all humanity!

Jesus knew all along what Peter's life *and* your life *and* my life *in Christ* ... *in Him* ... would mean.

As I imagine Jesus hanging ... being crucified ... on that cross ... my heart is flooded with vivid scenes of the love and power of God — the holy torture of Jesus is mixed with the forgiving, holy dripping blood of Jesus!

These scenes of horror *and* victory fill my mind again and again ... as the Holy Spirit describes to me Jesus with Peter — both crucified!

My flesh body grows hot and weakens ... my mind ... my heart ... my eyes fill with tears of pain and joy as I realize *we were crucified with Christ*!

"I have been crucified with Christ (in Him I have shared His crucifixion); it is no longer I who live, but Christ (the Messiah) lives in me; and the life I now live in the body I live by faith in (by adherence to and reliance on and complete trust in) the Son of God, Who loved me and gave Himself up for me." Galatians 2:20

My spirit ... my heart ... soars to rejoicing ... rejoicing ... rejoicing!

Oh the joy of receiving ... knowing our victorious Lord Jesus Who loves us and gave Himself up for all of us!

Oh the joy of walking ... filled ... with Jesus! Oh the joy to deeply listen to and talk with Jesus ... in the joy ... the power of the love of Jesus!

I know you can see God longs to bless you — He planned long ago for you to *know* and *receive* His great blessings to receive His love and His joy for you!

He longs for you to be His beloved blessing on this earth!

Jesus longs to show you His mercy ... His grace ... His forgiveness — He longs for you to *receive,* to *have* and for you to *give* His *unlimited* joy and love!

The New Testament is filled to over flow with God's joy, His love and His Great Hand of blessings on mankind!

God planned from before the beginning of time to bless Peter's worldwide ministry work!

God planned for Peter to be His blessing ... He always planned to build His Church ... on His faith ... and His love ... *in* Peter!

Jesus knew that Peter had the God-kind of faith ... the God love ...! Matthew 16:18, 19

Jesus said to Peter in Matthew 16:18, " *... I tell you, you are Peter (Greek, Petros — a large piece of rock), and on this rock (Greek, petra — a huge rock like Gibraltar) I will build My church, and the gates of Hades (the powers of the infernal region) shall not overpower it (or be strong to its detriment or hold out against it). I will give you the keys of the kingdom of heaven ...."*

Jesus told Peter that his very name means *"a large piece of rock"*. Then Jesus said, *" on this huge rock I will build My church, and even the gates of Hades (the powers of the infernal region) shall not overpower it ...."*

Beloved, the plans of God can not be overpowered!

But, by our not cooperating with God in His victorious, divine plans for us ... we can delay and alter the outcome of God's plans for our life!

> **Powerful God created you …**
> **to honor Him …**
> **to bless you …**
> ***and* He plans for you**
> **to be His blessing …**
> **throughout your life …**
> **across this earth!**

God answers prayer … God is willing to listen to you and to place His abilities and His love to complete His plans in your heart *through Jesus*!

Beloved, it is time! It is time for me … for you … for all of us … to turn … to *receive* … *receive* … all of God's greatest blessings He desires for us … is it time for us to turn … to *receive* … to agree to be the greatest blessing for God that He plans and that He created us to be!

My heart rejoices as I read — as I hear in my spirit — the loving, faith filled forgiving words of Jesus … filled with God's grace and His mercy of forgiveness! As I hear His divine call of power to all mankind on the earth I have no doubt …

… each one of us, in some special way or another … are all blessed and victoriously called by God!

> **We can honor Father God …**
> ***receive* His blessings**
> ***and* be the greatest blessing**
> **God created us to be!**

This is the time of the ages to honor God ... to turn ... to *receive* ALL God's goodness in all the love of Jesus ... to joyfully give away ALL the goodness ... that He is ... to ALL!

Have you ever listened to, or lived in, the devil's suggestions (lies) ... listened long enough to make you feel fearful and make you think you are a failure ... long enough to make you think or feel that all you have done ... or not done ... makes you not good enough for God to bless you or use you to be His blessing?

Let's be frank ... in ignorance we all have!

Right now, receive and understand ...

GOD IS LOVE! HE EXTRAVANGTLY LOVES! GOD GAVE US HIS EXTRAVAGNAT LOVE IN JESUS AS HIS ULTIMATE BLESSING!

> **Receiving Jesus gives us right of ownership to every blessing of God!**

JESUS IS LORD ...

JESUS IS LOVE!

Satan (*not God)*, is in the "faith sifting" ... "faith tearing down" ... "faith destroying" ... "mark you off" ... "faith and joy killing" business!

This is the devil's mission ... his whole purpose is to deceive ... to kill ... to steal ... to destroy every good thing of God!

Satan is Evil! He is a "faith sifter" ... Satan is the Killer ... the Thief ... the Devil ... the Evil of all evil!
John 10:10

It is the devil's mission to steal, kill and destroy! And remember, the only way Satan can steal, kill, and destroy is ... **when we let him**!

And one tragic way we let Satan steal, kill and destroy is by not joyfully *receiving* all of God's goodness and victorious blessings! Then, we lose out even greater by not being God's great blessings across this earth!

But beloved, mission or not ... Satan, the loser, *is already* defeated ... 2,000 years ago ... *you can keep him out of your life!*

Make it a practice to NEVER hang out with a loser!

"(God) disarmed the principalities and powers that were ranged against us and made a bold display and public example of them, in triumphing over them in Him and in it (the cross)."
Colossians 2:15

God, our *good* Father, has triumphed over the devil and every demon from hell *in Jesus* ... *and* He has *good* plans for you ... good, good plans ... God victoriously believes in you!
Jeremiah 29:11

GOD IS THE GREAT "faith builder"!

**Our Father God *is* The Greatest
"faith builder"
"faith protector"
"faith keeper"**

**Our Father God is in the "believing" …
"providing" … "healing" …
"joy of the Lord" … business!**

Jesus is God's greatest main good plan for you!

Jesus is alive and full of joy … full of good today … right now … for you!

You can completely trust Jesus and God's powerful Word in His Holy Sprit to protect you … to lead you.

You can act on God's Word! You can watch Him work for your good on your behalf.

Jesus said, *"Go then and make disciples of all nations, baptizing them into the name of the Father and of the Son and of the Holy Spirit. Teaching them to observe everything that I have commanded you … behold I am with you …*

Go into all the world and preach and publish openly the good news (the Gospel) to every creature (of the whole human race) … in My name drive out demons … speak in new languages … lay hands on the sick and they will get well … He sat down at the right hand of God … the Lord kept working with them and confirming the message by the attesting signs and miracles."
Matthew 28:19, 20; Mark 16:15-20

Yes beloved, Jesus is alive ... for you ...
Today — now! He is alive for those you love ...
sitting at the right hand of the Father.

Jesus is with you ... asking you to teach all nations to
observe everything He has commanded you ...
asking you to go into all the world ...

To preach ...
To publish openly the good news ...
To every creature ...
To drive out demons ...
To speak in new languages ...
To lay hands on the sick and they get well ...

To know that He is working with you
confirming His message
by the attesting signs and miracles!

Start right now praising God ... rejoicing
rejoicing ... and keep on rejoicing!

Keep on praising Him and rejoicing until your body and mind are well. Keep on rejoicing until you're so full of the strength of God and His might and power that nothing can stop you.

Rejoice until every chain of bondage the devil has used to bind you snaps apart like a thin piece of thread!

Rejoice until people who pass by you on the street start talking to you ... and they will!

Rejoice — and keep on rejoicing about what makes you so joyful!

Rejoice! Feast on God everyday! Rejoice — enjoy — feasting on God in His powerful Word *one day at a time*!

Sail on out into the deepest waters of victory rejoicing in God's freedom and His glory until He returns for you!

With all my heart ... I believe ... God wants us to go rejoicing ... so filled with His Glory until He returns ... so filled with His Word that He shines through us as great beacons of light in the darkest of moments!

Rejoice ... rejoice ... it is Jesus — God's Word that will uphold you ... it is God's Word that will sustain you!
John 1:1

Listen to God ...

Receive all that He is — *joyfully receive* His loving, powerful Word ... *joyfully give* all that He is!

GO with Jesus!

Live in Jesus ... walk victoriously ... every day ... in Jesus ... live in His joy and in His excellent love for you in the integrity of His Word!

Go every day — enjoying — feasting on God one day at a time!

MY PRAYER FOR YOU — *"Holy Father ... I praise You that You alone are our Lord and Savior. I praise You Lord that with You, we are victorious over the earth ... over every circumstance in our lives ... over all universe's.*

I pray the seeds of Your Word's set themselves deep within the heart of every reader, every ear that is listening! Lord, I praise You that I can fully expect You to perform Your Word and bring every heart to maturity in Your love that hears You.

In the powerful name of Jesus I stand victoriously with You Lord on behalf of those who are seeking Your face ... that they may see You quickly with great peace and rest as they go to give Your joy and freedom to a sick and dying world!"

Love,

ROSE

JESUS IS LORD
JESUS IS LOVE

"For (during) forty days in the wilderness (desert), where He was tempted (tried, tested exceedingly) by the devil. And He ate nothing during those days, and when they were completed, He was hungry.

Then the devil said to Him, If You are the Son of God, order this stone to turn into a loaf (of bread).

And Jesus replied to him, It is written, Man shall not live and be sustained by (on) bread alone but by every word and expression of God."   Luke 4:2-4

Enjoying FEASTING on GOD

One Day at a Time

is one of the most important things
you will ever do for your life and your loved ones!

Get rid of fear, doubt, worry and unbelief — !

For encouragement, *unlimited* joy and love —
keep going — keep giving — sowing this book
of freedom, love and victorious living
into the life of a friend and a loved one!

NOTES

Prayer for Salvation
and Baptism in the Holy Spirit

Heavenly Father, I come to You in the Name of Jesus. Your Word says, *"Whosoever shall call on the name of the Lord shall be saved"* in Acts 2:21 … so I call on You Lord.

I pray Father, asking Jesus to come into my heart, and be Lord over my life, according to Romans 10:9 *"Because if you acknowledge and confess with your lips that Jesus is Lord and in your heart believe that God raised Him from the dead, you will be saved."*

I do that now. I confess with my mouth that Jesus is Lord and I believe in my heart that God raised Him from the dead. I am now re-born — re-created! I am a Christian — a child of Almighty God! I receive my salvation! I am saved!

You also said in Your Word Lord, *"If you then, evil as you are, know how to give good gifts to your children, how much more will your heavenly Father give the Holy Spirit to those who ask and continue to ask Him!"* Luke 11:13

Lord, I am also asking You to fill me with the Holy Spirit. *"Holy Spirit, rise up within me as I praise God. I fully expect to speak with other tongues as You give me utterance."* Amen   Acts 2:4

Begin now to praise God! Praise Him for filling you with His Love and His Holy Spirit. Let your voice rise up in praise to Father God in the voice the Holy Spirit gives you. Use your voice to worship and praise Him in heavenly language.

Make every day a day of blessing! Father God has given you the great blessing of His Love, His mercy, forgiveness and life eternal with Him. You are a born again, recreated, Spirit-filled believer. You'll never be the same!

Now, find a strong, good Word of God, preaching church! Become a part of a church family who will love you and care for you as you care for them.

We need to be joined to each other. Like a tightly woven rope, it is God's plan for us to be strong in unity together.

Signed _____

Date _____

I praise my Father God!
I am saved, healed *and* made whole.

VICTORY PRODUCTS
Books, Tapes, & CD's Available from
Rose Leibundguth Ministries

GOD's COOKIN' *and the* ***DEVIL's*** **WELL DONE**
LOVE IS ON THE THRONE *and* HE's NOT NERVOUS
ENJOY FEASTING ON GOD — *One Day at a Time*
JESUS IS LOVE — *You Can Have That Chicken*
DANCING WITH *THE KING*
DRESSED TO WIN
KNOW WHO YOU ARE
GOD'S WILL FOR YOU
JESUS IS YOUR DEFENDER
THE DEVIL IS YOUR SLAVE
MERCY'S VOICE
SET FREE INDEED
PRAISE HIM INSTEAD

The Lone Ranger had a Tonto (unity in the community)
Holy Bologny (sit down — eat with Jesus)
ONE BABY's DEAD, but, FIVE ARE ALIVE (keep your eyes on Jesus)
When the Devil Presses in - YOU PRESS ON
You are More Than A Conqueror
Hunger to be Satisfied
Christ in You
SET FREE — SET FREE — SET FREE
Love Life is Worth Living
Patience is Consistent Faith
Love Overcomes Everything
You can Never Stumble or Fall
Cast Your Good Bread on the Water
Give More … MORE & MORE
Plant Seeds — Remove Pressure
What Being Rich Really Means
Fear Makes the Wolf Look Bigger Than He Is
Stop Trying to Become What You Already Are
Praise Him Instead
GO — GO — GO
Steer Clear from Big Failures
Leave that Past Behind
Already Healed
Warfare in the Spirit Realm
Get Tired of Worry and Defeat
Be Confident & Courageous
Love Takes Charge
Playing to Win with God

AND MORE!

We're Here for You

Rose Leibundguth Ministries

Ask about Partnership!
To receive RLM books and tapes
contact your local bookstore — sow hope and victory
into the lives of friends and loved ones
or
call 1-866-324-8447
(9 a.m. - 5 p.m. ET)

Write, Call or E-mail:

Rose Leibundguth Ministries
Burgin, KY 40310 ~ (859) 748-9961
e-mail home55@earthlink.net
www.mercyhouserocks.org

We're Here for You!

To receive more information about RLM and a FREE subscription to *Mercy's Voice of Victory* or if you are writing from outside the U.S., please contact the RLM office nearest you.

World Offices of Rose Leibundguth Ministries

Rose Leibundguth Ministries
Burgin, Kentucky 40310

Rose Leibundguth
% Joseph P. Ho
C&S, The Christian Shop Pte Ltd
No: 61 Stamford Road
#01-01 Stamford Court
Singapore 178892
Republic of SIGNAPORE

Rose Leibundguth
% Pastor Gether Mag-Usara
Don Luis Village
Mati Davao Oriental
8200 PHILIPPINES

Rose Leibundguth Ministries

Victory Vision

To bring the un-compromised
Word of God
to all who will hear.

Proclaiming the Good News
to all who will receive.

Challenging Christians to live in victory,
grow to maturity,
and develop to truly know
the perfect will of God
for their life!

To take Jesus and His powerful love
and God's Word to the world!

PARTNER INFORMATION

Covenant partnership is vital! Your success *is* Jesus — Jesus and your success *are* our priority!

Partnership immediately puts you directly on the field of action!

Partnership is dynamic — all powerful! Partnership is a powerful bond ... a two-sided relationship. *(Partnership, by definition, means to take a part in).* As Jesus said,

"I am the True Vine, and My Father is the Vinedresser ... you are the branch ... However apart from Me you can do nothing ... He ... repeatedly prunes every branch that continues to bear fruit, to make it bear ... richer *and* more excellent fruit ... when you bear (produce) much fruit, My Father is honored *and* glorified, and you show and prove yourselves to be true followers of Mine ... I have told you these things, that My joy and delight may be in you, and that your joy *and* gladness may be of full measure *and* complete *and* overflowing ... This is My commandment: that you love one another (just) as I have loved you." John 15:1, 5, 8, 11, 12

Every Partner of Rose Leibundguth Ministries has a dynamic, significant role in this ministry. God provides through each Partner's prayers — through their vital words of encouragement — support — God provides for what He is doing through each Partner's giving world-wide.

For your FREE partner tape and further information on how to become partner's with RLM, please contact us at our headquarter offices in Kentucky!

If this book has changed your life, we would like to hear from you. Please write us at:

Rose Leibundguth Ministries
Burgin, Kentucky 40310